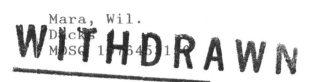

animals**animals**

Ducks

by **Wil Mara**

 **Marshall Cavendish**
Benchmark
New York

Thanks to Ted Woynicz, "The Duckman of D.C."—providing protection
and advocacy for wild waterfowl residing in
the Washington, D.C. urban region—for his expert reading of this manuscript.

Marshall Cavendish Benchmark
99 White Plains Road
Tarrytown, New York 10591-5502
www.marshallcavendish.us

Library of Congress Cataloging-in-Publication Data

Mara, Wil.
Ducks / by Wil Mara.
p. cm. — (Animals animals)
Summary: "Provides comprehensive information on the anatomy, special skills,
habitats, and diet of ducks"—Provided by publisher.
Includes index.
ISBN 978-0-7614-2927-2
1. Ducks—Juvenile literature. I. Title. II. Series.
QL696.A52M36 2008
598.4'1—dc22
2007026004

Photo research by Joan Meisel

Cover photo: Lynda Richardson/Corbis
The photographs in this book are used by permission and through the courtesy of:
AP Images: 36. *Alamy*: William Leaman, 24; Papilio, 27; Leslie Garland Picture Library, 33; Steven J. Kazlowski, 38;
Robert McGouey, 39. *Animals Animals - Earth Scenes*: Theo Allofs/zefa, 1; Mark Stouffer, 14; Henry Ausloos, 28.
Corbis: Herbert Spichtinger/zefa, 4; Kennan Ward, 6; Stephanie_Pilick/epa, 16; Carl & Ann Purcell, 19;
Lynda Richardson, 22, 40; Arctic-Images, 26; Joe McDonald, 30; Roger Tidman, 32. *drr.net*: Ann Howley, 10;
Ron Niebrugge/wildnatureimages, 12; C. Robert Smith, 13; Rob Palmer Photography, 20. *Getty Images*: Tom Vezo, 18;
Freudenthal Verhagen, 21. *Minden Pictures*: Jim Brandenburg, 17. *Peter Arnold Inc.*: D. Harms, 9; Markus Matzel, 34;
S. Stuewer, 41. *Photo Researchers, Inc.*: Gary Meszaros, 7.

Editor: Joy Bean
Publisher: Michelle Bisson
Art Director: Anahid Hamparian
Series Designer: Adam Mietlowski

Printed in Malaysia

1 3 5 6 4 2

Contents

1 Introducing the Duck

They whistle, they waddle, they dabble, and they dive—they are ducks, and they are among the most interesting creatures in the world. There are so many *species*, they have so many colors, and they have such fascinating habits. If you like birds, then you are likely a fan of the duck.

Ducks are part of a larger group of birds that includes swans and geese. Scientists call this group *Anatidae*. Members of this family are also called *waterfowl* because they spend so much of their time in water. Most ducks are smaller than other anatids. There are over a hundred different duck species worldwide.

Ducks come in many colors and sizes. Their unique waddle sets them apart from other birds.

Swans are part of the same family, Anatidae, as geese and ducks.

Ducks can be found on every continent except one—Antarctica—and on most of the world's islands. They live in a variety of climates, from warm tropical regions to chillier areas of the extreme north and south. As far as habitat is concerned, water is the key element. Some ducks prefer the fresh water of ponds and rivers, while others like the saltiness of oceans and some large lakes. A few species have been known to travel between both habitats. They can also be found in semiaquatic environments such as marshes and swampland.

As long as they are near water, ducks are happy.

A duck's body is specially built for life in the water. On land ducks walk, or waddle, in what appears to be a very uncomfortable way. This is because their legs are set well apart and are far back on their longish, oval-shaped bodies. When they are in the water, however, this peculiar arrangement serves them very well—their webbed feet are better able to propel them forward, making them excellent swimmers and, in some cases, divers.

Ducks also have *bills* that are modified to help them eat in the water. There are several different types. Some ducks have long, narrow bills with rows of tiny comblike projections running along the inside of the bill. These projections are called *lamellae*. When a duck picks food out of the water, the lamellae trap the food inside its mouth while the water drains out. Other ducks have shorter and more powerful bills, which can be used to crack open hard-shelled items like clams and mollusks. A few ducks have bills with sharp edges, which enable them to slice through tough prey like large fish. A duck's nostrils are located far back from the top of its bill, which allows the duck to dabble in shallow water and breathe comfortably at the same time.

Webbed feet help ducks move swiftly through the water.

A duck's outer feathers are often colorful and beautifully patterned.

A duck has two layers of feathers—inner and outer. The inner layer, called *down*, is the softer of the two and actually consists of several layers. It traps air to keep the animal warm in the water. The outer layer is what keeps a duck "waterproof." This is done with the help of oil that comes from a gland at the base of the duck's tail. A duck will rub this oil all over its feathers with its bill several times a day. Ducks have wings as well, although some species are unable to actually fly.

Since there are so many different duck species, they vary greatly in color. The males, which are called *drakes*, are generally more colorful than the females. Males are often colored with beautiful reds, blues, and greens. Most females, on the other hand, are a duller color, such as brown or gray. They are often called *hens*.

Species Chart

General Characteristics

◆ **Length (body):** 12 to 28 inches (30.5 to 71 cm)

◆ **Weight:** 10 ounces to 6 pounds (0.28 to 2.7 kg)

◆ **Height (ground to top of head):** 10 to 15 inches (25.4 to 38.1 cm)

A male duck with colorful feathers.

A female duck usually has more neutral coloring.

◆ **Coloration:** Varies by species and gender. Males tend to be more colorful, e.g., black or grey with blues, greens, or reds. Females have more earth tones, e.g., brown or gray in order to blend with their surroundings and go unnoticed by predators. Bill color varies widely and includes white, black, green, orange, yellow, and brown.

◆ **Life Span:** Three to five years in the wild up to twenty-five years in captivity with proper care.

Did You Know . . .
Not all ducks are able to fly. Some, like the Falkland steamer duck, have wings that are too small to keep them up in the air. When they are alarmed, they can leap from the ground and flap around for a few seconds, but that is all. Flightless ducks are often more vulnerable to predators because of their inability to take to the air to escape.

2 How Ducks Live

Ducks can be noisy creatures. The sound that most people are familiar with is their raspy quack, but they make other sounds, too—most commonly a variety of whistles, chirps, or low grunts. They do so for many different reasons—when they are frightened, when they want to attract a mate, or when they are searching for food. Sometimes they are trying to warn other ducks that danger is nearby.

Ducks spend much of their time eating. This is because flying and mating requirc a great deal of energy, so their bodies need as much nutrition as possible. Ducks are either *divers* or *dabblers*. Diving ducks go fully underwater to retrieve food, while dabblers usually only skim the surface.

A duck's unique quack is just one of the noises it makes.

This dabbler duck is searching for food while its back end stays afloat.

A dabbler will sometimes stick its head under water to dig something out of the mud, as long as the water is not too deep. When it reaches down, the back half of its body will remain out of the water, with its tail up in the air. Divers are generally heavier than dabblers, which makes it easier for them to submerge themselves (but more difficult for them to fly). Some ducks also search for food around the edges of water along muddy shorelines.

Most ducks are *omnivorous*, meaning they will eat both plants and animals. Dabblers eat more plant matter, including many waterweeds, green algae, and

A diver duck goes completely underwater to search for food.

Some ducks eat hard-shelled items. This duck, for example, is feeding on a clam.

grasses, plus different types of seeds. However, they will also eat any insects or tiny aquatic animals (such as fish and small frogs) that cross their path. Diving ducks prefer creatures that are easy to catch, such as worms, clams, mollusks, crayfish, crabs, large insects, and a variety of fish. They will, however, just as happily eat hearty plants, even pulling them out by the roots. Ducks that live in the oceans and seas can catch fairly large fish. Their bills have sharp, serrated edges, which make it easy for them to catch, carry, and cut up their meals. They also eat clams, mollusks, and other hard-shelled prey.

Along with food, a duck also swallows small stones and particles of grit. These items then go to a special organ inside its body called a *gizzard*. The gizzard does what our teeth do—it grinds up the food so it can be digested easily. Inside the gizzard, the stones and grit roll around, aided by the movement of surrounding muscles, and slowly wear down the food into tiny pieces. These pieces then move on to the duck's true stomach, and digestion begins. Once the gizzard stones become too smooth to perform their function, the duck will throw them up and find new ones.

Ducks also find food on land. They eat different types of grasses and seeds.

*When the weather turns colder or food has become
scarce, ducks migrate to a better location.*

Did You Know . . .
Migrating ducks often
return to the same areas—
for breeding in the spring
and resting in the winter—
year after year. They are able
to follow their course by
recognizing landmarks along
the ground (such as rivers,
mountains, and highways)
and the stars in the night sky.

Once a year, ducks in colder regions of the
world travel southward to find warmer
places to live temporarily. This process is
called *migration*. They leave in the fall,
when it begins to grow cold and food items
become harder to find. They usually
migrate during daylight hours, but occa-
sionally they fly during the night. Ducks
migrate in flocks, often flying in a V-
shaped pattern or in a single line.
Depending on the species and where they

start their migration, ducks can travel hundreds or even over two thousand miles to reach their wintering sites. The flocks may make several stops along the way, to find food and to rest. Once they reach their destination, they continue eating and resting.

Migration flights often cover 400 to 500 miles (644 to 805 km) in a single day. Ducks can lose 25 to 50 percent of their body weight during this flight, and it can take two weeks or more for them to regain the fat reserves they lost. In the spring, when they have regained enough energy, they fly north again and begin another breeding season.

Migrating ducks often fly in a V-shaped pattern.

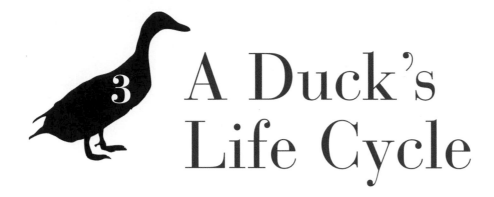

3 A Duck's Life Cycle

The life cycle of a duck usually begins at the start of winter, when a female searches for a mate. Males are just as eager to form this partnership, and they will perform several *courting* gestures in order to get a female's attention. A male will already stand out because of his brightly colored feathers, but he may also make a variety of noises (grunts and whistles), bob his head up and down, ruffle his feathers, splash in the water, and even chase a female through the air, sometimes nipping at her tail feathers. Several males may go after the same female, in which case fighting may occur. The males will quack, flap, and snap at each other, although rarely will they cause each other

Two male ducks trying to get a female's attention.

23

These duck eggs have been laid in a nest of feathers and grass.

serious injuries. Once a female decides which male will be her mate, the pair stays together until all their ducklings have hatched.

The female carries the developing eggs inside her body for thirty to forty-five days. During this time she builds a nest, usually within clumps of grass or tall weeds, in a spot that is not far from water and is well hidden. She builds the nest from leaves and bits of grass, and also from down feathers that she plucks from her body—usually her chest and belly. Then she lays anywhere from five to fifteen oval-shaped eggs. She sits on the eggs to keep them warm and to guard them. If she has to leave the nest, she will cover the eggs so that *predators* (animals that hunt ducks and their eggs) cannot see them. Such animals include foxes, squirrels, snakes, raccoons, and large birds.

A baby duck grows quickly inside the egg. It is ready to hatch in about a month. It breaks through the shell with the help of a tiny tooth at the tip of its bill. This is called an *egg tooth*, and it falls off shortly after the duck hatches. A duckling is covered in soft, downy feathers, giving it a fuzzy appearance. At this point the male duck has left, and the mother must care for the young on her own. She keeps the duckings warm as they snuggle against her body and under her wings. Then she leads them to the water, where she teaches them to swim and to find food.

A mother duck sits on her eggs to keep them safe and warm.

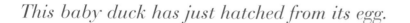

This baby duck has just hatched from its egg.

Ducklings grow quickly, losing their baby feathers in a few weeks and gaining their adult feathers after nine to twelve weeks. They are able to fly by the end of their third month.

Did You Know . . .
The female duck chooses the breeding and nesting site—a choice that is based largely on where she has successfully nested before and possibly the general area in which she herself hatched.

*A mother leads her ducklings to water in order to teach them
how to swim and find food.*

28

Over the summer they continue to grow rapidly. In this same period, the adult ducks lose their flying feathers in a process called *molting*. They must find a safe place to stay while the new set of feathers develops. The males also lose the colorful feathers they had at the end of the previous winter, when they were trying to attract the attention of the females. These bright colors do not return until the fall, when they molt again in preparation for the next breeding season.

As winter arrives, both the adults and the young leave the breeding area (if necessary) and migrate south to a warmer climate. At the end of winter, the breeding cycle begins again.

4 Survival in the Wild

Surviving in nature is not easy for any animal, and some have a tougher time than others. Ducks are not exactly rugged, so they are an easy target for predators. Since they live in and around bodies of water, their most common predators are found there as well. Alligators and crocodiles have been known to grab ducks right off the water's surface. Large fish will eat a duck if it is small enough. Ducks also have to watch out for powerful and aggressive birds, such as hawks and eagles. They go after full-grown ducks without hesitation—but they just as eagerly attack ducklings, too.

It is interesting to note that some animals actually *help* ducks survive. Studies in some areas have

Alligators include ducks and other water birds in their diet.

A mother duck protects her chicks from attack.

shown, for example, that coyotes hunt animals that normally prey on ducks. As a result, the ducks in that area will thrive as long as there are coyotes around to "protect" them.

Human beings have always been a great threat to ducks. Perhaps the most threatening practice these days is *habitat destruction*. This is the process of humans destroying the places that ducks call home.

32

For example, if a pond is drained and then filled in so something can be built on the land, that is habitat destruction. The ducks that lived there now have no place to search for food, to make nests, or to raise their young. They must find another place to live. A second form of habitat destruction involves dumping garbage and other waste products into natural areas.

A duck swims in polluted water.

Did You Know . . .

Duck hunters often use fake ducks to attract the attention of real ones. In years past these fakes, called decoys, were made of wood and painted with bright colors. Duck decoys are often prized by naturalists as collectibles.

This duck is getting special care. Workers clean the duck after it was caught in an oil spill.

If the water becomes dirty or poisoned, large numbers of ducks can die simply from swimming in it. Their food items could also suddenly become dangerous for them to eat. Oil spills in the oceans also kill thousands of ducks and other birds related to them.

Humans have also hunted ducks for centuries. Some hunters shoot them for sport. Ducks are also hunted for their meat. Duck meat is popular in many restaurants, even though it is greasy and not very healthy. Duck feathers—particularly down—are used to make everything from warm clothing to pillows.

5 The Future of the Duck

As the human population grows and wetland habitats are destroyed by new houses and stores being built, more ducks and other animals are forced to seek out new places to live. Ducks have one advantage over most wild creatures in this respect—they can fly. It is a fairly simple matter for them to leave one area in search of another (provided they are not caring for their young at the time). The problem, however, is finding a new spot that is just right—one that provides not only clean water but also an abundance of food and places for them to build nests and hide from predators.

A mother and her ducklings search for a place to live.

Some ducks, like the Steller's Eiders in Alaska, are endangered and need help from conservation groups.

Did You Know . . .

A duck known as the Madagascar pochard was once thought to be extinct but has since been rediscovered. Scientists feared the species had disappeared by the early 1900s. Then, in November 2006, nine adults and four ducklings were found in a small pond in the northern part of Madagascar.

There are many *conservation groups* dedicated to protecting ducks and other waterfowl. Their greatest priority is to preserve the land on which the birds live. A skilled hunter can kill only a few ducks a day, but a bulldozer plowing down hundreds of acres of forest will, in the long run, cause the death of thousands of animals. Conservation groups raise money in order to buy untouched land, then protect it from any efforts to build on it. Similarly, they lobby, or petition, their governments to declare certain areas off-limits to builders.

Governments also help by including rare duck breeds in their endangered species programs. Once an animal is put on the endangered species list, it cannot be hunted, trapped, or otherwise harmed. Doing this would be breaking the law, and the penalties can be severe. Also, the habitat in which the species lives can be protected, and plans are made to find ways to aid its recovery. Unfortunately, endangered species programs do not exist in all countries. Also, it is difficult to make sure such laws are obeyed. For example, if someone is deep in the woods alone and shooting at ducks in a little pond, how would anyone else know? How could the hunter be stopped?

Once endangered, the harlequin duck has made something of a comeback thanks to an increase in wild populations.

Captive-breeding programs have helped bring many animals back from near *extinction*. Extinction is the point at which a species disappears forever. Rare duck species can be bred under controlled conditions, in which the parents are kept clean and well fed,

To keep some species of ducks from going extinct, captive-breeding programs keep duck eggs safe in nesting boxes like the one seen here.

and the eggs are *incubated* and hatched indoors, away from predators. Common duck species are also bred on farms for their meat, eggs, or feathers. Because of these farming programs, wild flocks can be left alone.

The future of wild ducks will always be uncertain. There are many different duck species, and some are becoming very rare. The key to ensuring their survival is simply making an effort to protect them, and that is up to us—people in government, people in conservation groups, and everyone else. As long as people continue to care—and the ducks remain able to adapt to an ever-changing world—they should survive. But only time will tell for sure.

Glossary

Anatidae—The animal family that includes ducks, geese, and swans.

bill—The hard, protruding part of a duck's mouth, used to catch and cut up food items.

captive-breeding program—A program designed to allow animals to breed safely in a controlled environment, usually for the purpose of sustaining a species that is in danger of becoming extinct.

conservation group—An organization dedicated to the protection of wild plants and animals.

courting—Displays made by male ducks (drakes) to attract the attention of female ducks (hens) at the start of the breeding season.

dabbler—A duck that finds most of its food on or just under the water's surface.

diver—A duck that dives under the water's surface to secure its food, often from the muddy bottoms of oceans or from freshwater ponds and lakes.

down—The soft, inner layer of feathers on a duck's body.

drake—A male duck.

egg tooth—A sharp, tiny tooth used by ducklings to cut their way out of their shells during hatching. It falls off shortly after they hatch.

extinction—The state of no longer existing.

gizzard—A special organ inside a duck's body that grinds food so it can be easily digested. It performs the same function as a human's teeth.

habitat destruction—The elimination or ruination of natural areas, such that animals that lived there must find new places to live.

hen—A female duck or other bird.

incubate—To promote the development and hatching of an animal's eggs by keeping them at a suitable temperature.

lamellae—Comblike projections that run in a row along the inside of a duck's bill.

migration—The practice of traveling long distances to avoid local shortages of food, usually caused by winter cold. Animals return to their original homes the following spring, when the weather is warm again and there is more food available.

molt—To shed old feathers so they can be replaced by new ones.

omnivorous—Eating both plants and animals.

predator—An animal that eats other animals for food.

species—A group of living things that share the same characteristics and mate only with their own kind.

waterfowl—A bird that lives primarily in the water.

Find Out More

Books

Hall, Margaret. *Ducks and Their Ducklings* (Animal Offspring). Mankato, MN: Capstone Press, 2004.

Hall, Margaret. *Mallards* (Wetland Animals). Mankato, MN: Capstone Press, 2006.

Higginson, Mel. *Migration* (Nature's Cycles). Vero Beach, FL: Rourke Publishing, 2007.

Hudak, Heather. *Ducks* (Farm Animals). New York: Weigl Publishers, 2006.

Petty, Kate. *Ducklings* (Baby Animals). Mankato, MN: Stargazer Books, 2005.

Web Sites

Animal Diversity Web pages for the Anatidae family
http://animaldiversity.ummz.umich.edu/site/
accounts/information/Anatidae.html

Ducks Unlimited home page—an organization
dedicated to duck conservation
http://www.ducks.org

KiddyHouse page for ducks—includes activities
http://www.kiddyhouse.com/Farm/ducks1.html

National Geographic page for all birds—very kid-
friendly with lots of great photos and
information
http://animals.nationalgeographic.com/
animals/birds.html?nav=TOPNAV

Index

Page numbers for illustrations are in **boldface**.

About the Author

Wil Mara is the author of more than eighty books, many of which are reference titles for young readers. More information about his work can be found at www.wilmara.com